Dear Parent:
Your child's love of reading starts here!

Every child learns to read in a different way and at his or her own speed. Some go back and forth between reading levels and read favorite books again and again. Others read through each level in order. You can help your young reader improve and become more confident by encouraging his or her own interests and abilities. From books your child reads with you to the first books he or she reads alone, there are I Can Read Books for every stage of reading:

SHARED READING
Basic language, word repetition, and whimsical illustrations, ideal for sharing with your emergent reader

BEGINNING READING
Short sentences, familiar words, and simple concepts for children eager to read on their own

READING WITH HELP
Engaging stories, longer sentences, and language play for developing readers

READING ALONE
Complex plots, challenging vocabulary, and high-interest topics for the independent reader

ADVANCED READING
Short paragraphs, chapters, and exciting themes for the perfect bridge to chapter books

I Can Read Books have introduced children to the joy of reading since 1957. Featuring award-winning authors and illustrators and a fabulous cast of beloved characters, I Can Read Books set the standard for beginning readers.

A lifetime of discovery begins with the magical words "I Can Read!"

Visit www.icanread.com for information on enriching your child's reading experience.

I Can Read!™ SHARED My First READING

Axel THE TRUCK

Rocky Road

Story by **J. D. Riley**

Pictures by **Brandon Dorman**

Greenwillow Books, *An Imprint of* HarperCollins*Publishers*

Adobe Illustrator was used to prepare the full-color art.
I Can Read Book® is a trademark of HarperCollins Publishers.

Axel the Truck: Rocky Road. Copyright © 2011 by HarperCollins Publishers.
First published as an ebook, 2011; first hardcover and paperback publication, 2013.
All rights reserved. No part of this book may be used or reproduced in any
manner whatsoever without written permission except in the case of brief quotations
embodied in critical articles and reviews. Printed in the United States of America.
For information address HarperCollins Children's Books, a division of
HarperCollins Publishers, 195 Broadway, New York, NY 10007.
www.icanread.com

Library of Congress Cataloging-in-Publication Data
Riley, J. D.
Axel the truck : rocky road / story by J. D. Riley ; pictures by Brandon Dorman.
pages cm
"Greenwillow Books."
Summary: Axel the truck zooms up a rocky, twisty mountain road.
ISBN 978-0-06-222232-9 (hardcover)—ISBN 978-0-06-222231-2 (pbk.)
[1. Trucks—Fiction. 2. Mountains—Fiction.] I. Dorman, Brandon, illustrator.
II. Title. III. Title: Rocky road.
PZ7.R453Ax 2013 [E]—dc23 2013012764

16 17 18 PC/WOR 10 9 8 7 6 5 4 3 2

Greenwillow Books

For Mom and her red truck back home
—J. D. R.

For Uncle Steve
—B. D.

Axel is a red truck.

Axel has big, big wheels.

7

"I like to go fast," Axel says.

Vroom, vroom, varoom!

Zip, zip, zoom!

"Bumpy roads are best,"
Axel says.
Bang, bang, bump!

Axel rolls down the road.
He rolls past the town.

Axel's big tires spin around.
Zip, zip, zoom!

"I like to climb," Axel says.
Up the mountain Axel goes.

Zig, zag, zig, zag.

Axel races a mountain goat.

Vroom, vroom, varoom!

Go, go, go!

Axel speeds around a bend.

Axel jets off a steep hill.

He flies over the trail.
"Yahoo!" Axel says.

Axel blasts his horn.

Beep, beep, beep!

Down the mountain Axel goes.

Axel catches a falling rock.

Thump, thump, whump!

Axel carries a rocky load.

He carts it to the dump.

Vroom, vroom, varoom!

Bump, bump, clunk!

Beep, beep, beep!

Time for a pit stop.

Axel's big tires spin around.

Axel races back to town.

Vroom, varoom!

Zip, zip, zoom!

That was monster fun.

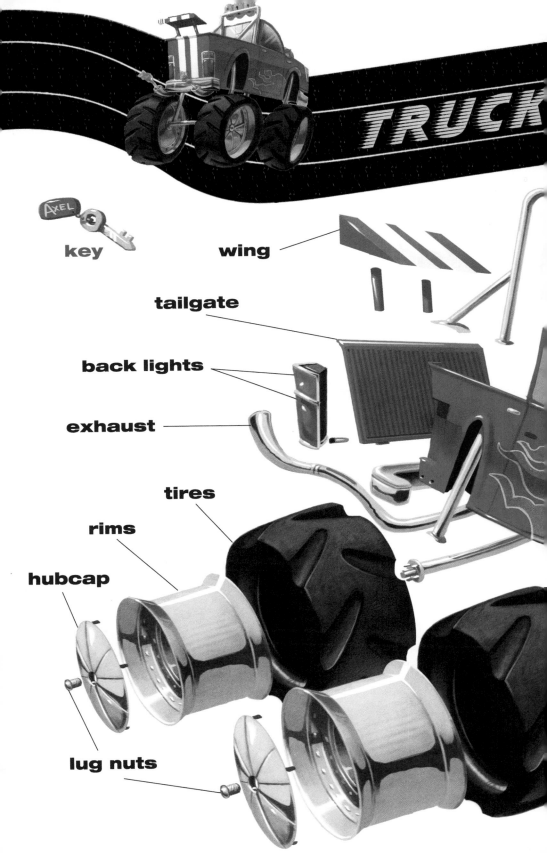

TRUCK

key

wing

tailgate

back lights

exhaust

tires

rims

hubcap

lug nuts

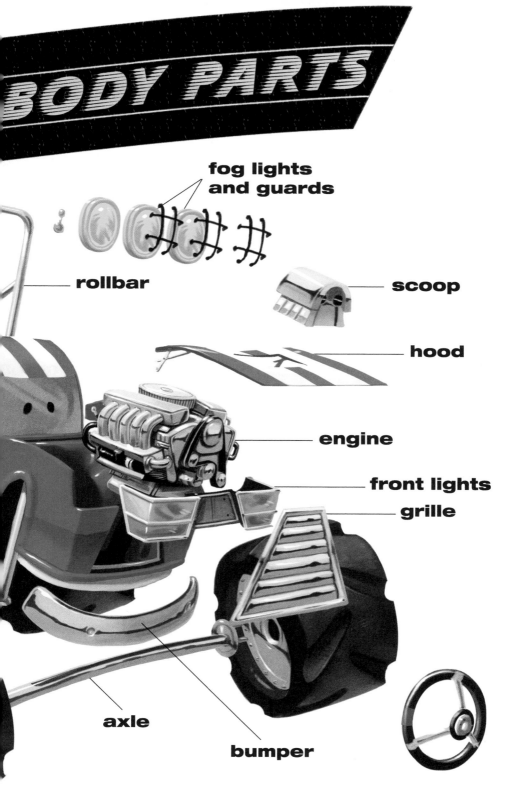

BODY PARTS

fog lights and guards

rollbar

scoop

hood

engine

front lights

grille

axle

bumper

steering wheel

TOOLS

screwdriver

pliers

wrenches

flashlight

bolt

socket wrench

spark plug

lug wrench

drill